The Great Race

Written by Lisa Thompson

Pictures by Craig Smith and Lew Keilar

Captain Red Beard was excited. The Great Pirate Race was tomorrow.

The crew had been training for weeks. The Black Beast was sure to win.

2

All the ships in the race had to sail out
of Pirate Cove, around Skull Rock and
back to port.

A dozen ships had entered the race.

The first one back to port would be the winner.

The prize was a treasure chest full of gold.

Every pirate from Pirate Cove wanted to win.

Captain Red Beard and his crew were ready. The gun went off, the race was on.

A gust of wind filled The Black Beast's sails.

The ship raced into the lead.

"Get ready to collect our treasure," said the Captain.

The Black Beast sailed nearer and nearer to Skull Rock. It was a dangerous spot. Many ships were wrecked on its reefs. The crew could see the broken ships in the water. Suddenly, there was a giant BOOM near the ship.

"Shiver me topsails!" cried Captain Red Beard. "That was a cannonball."

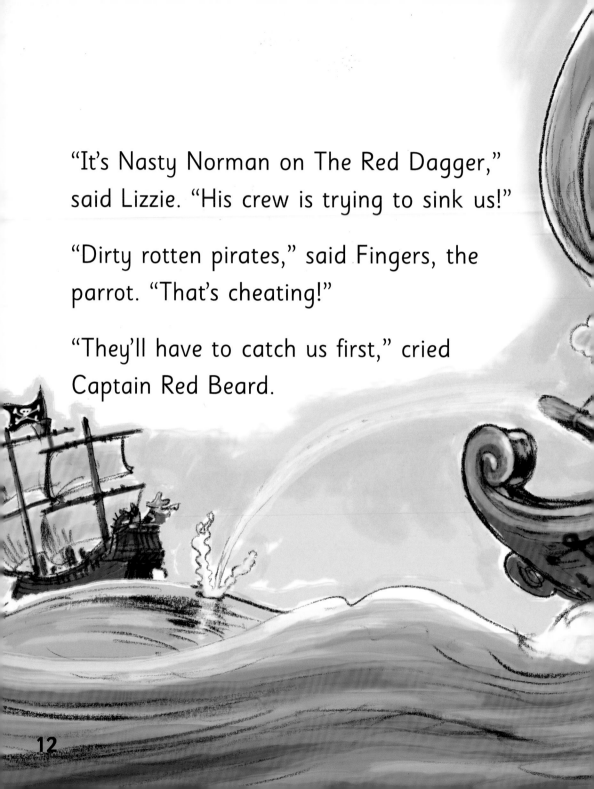

"It's Nasty Norman on The Red Dagger," said Lizzie. "His crew is trying to sink us!"

"Dirty rotten pirates," said Fingers, the parrot. "That's cheating!"

"They'll have to catch us first," cried Captain Red Beard.

Captain Red Beard steered The Black Beast towards Skull Rock.

"Captain! What are you doing? We'll sink on the rocks!" said Lizzie.

Nasty Norman and his crew followed
The Black Beast.

Boom! Boom! Boom!

Cannonballs flew from The Red Dagger.

Their cannons made a lot of smoke.

Captain Red Beard smiled.

He steered The Black Beast away
from Skull Rock.

He had sailed these seas many times.

Nasty Norman and his crew couldn't see where they were going. There was too much smoke around The Red Dagger.

They sailed right into Skull Rock.

The Black Beast sailed into Pirate Cove in first place. Captain Red Beard collected the winner's treasure.

But the real prize was watching Nasty Norman and his crew swim back to shore.